The American Patriot
&
Christianity

The collision of two ideals

Written by:
Michael "Mickey" Wilcox
January 2016

The American Patriot & Christianity

The American Patriot & Christianity

Honor, Loyalty, & Duty

Why write this short book? For starters, many American Christians are through and through patriots. They love the United States of America. More then that, they recognize that the Christian church in the United States does more to physically and economically advance the Gospel then any other nation. The United States no longer being a free republic would adversely affect that. In the past, we have found that American patriotism and Christianity could co-exist with little or no strife. However, in today's changing climate of policies and culture, the American Christian would be wise to take a step back and evaluate from a biblical perspective whether the two can co-exist or if a choice must be made.

"Every good citizen makes his country's honor his own, and cherishes it not only as a precious but as sacred. He is willing to risk his life in its defense and is conscious that he gains protection while he gives it." - Andrew Jackson

These days and times are difficult here in America for a Christian. It is politically incorrect to be a Bible believing, Christ following Christian. Oh, you can be a Christian. Just as long as you are willing to accept everybody else's philosophy as truth, understanding that "my truth may be different then your truth" and "we are all apart of the human race and beings of this world", "simply respect each others truth and love and affirm your fellow human". This truth by eliminating truth and making all things true actually makes me sick in my stomach to even write. There is always what is true and what is not true. Discerning truth may be difficult, but truth is still truth.

Over generations the church has fought compromise, false doctrine, and skewed theology. Many have come calling themselves "Christian," but when their actions and theology are stood next to the Holy Scriptures, we find that they are fakes, frauds, and anti-Christs. Here in America and the American church we have suffered the same struggles. We have seen polluted philosophies of hate, discrimination, and prosperity. The struggle is not that you are side-lined and useless when your doctrine of faith is found to be corrupt, the struggle is recognition, repentance, and renewed walk with Jesus. Today is no different. America and the American way of life, including our constitution is under attack and may very well fall. For the American church this offers a challenging look at who we are and how we must interact in our own country. In fact, this very topic has been weighing heavily upon me for a very long time and in these last 7 years it has come to a point where I have faced many sleepless nights and long debates with people as to who the Church is to be in the times that set directly upon our horizon.

"It cannot be emphasized to strongly or to often that this great nation was founded not by religionists, but by Christians; not on religions but on the Gospel of Jesus Christ. For that reason alone, people of other faiths have been afforded freedom of worship here." - Patrick Henry, American Patriot

A Little Background

I've long been an anti - "Bible believing, flag waving, gun-toting" Christian. Aside from the fact that it just never sat well with me, this very non-Christian behavior created an illusion that Christianity was an American religion. This of course, is far from the truth. Christianity is simply to be Christ-like; to follow the ways and teachings of Christ. However, my Christianity has never stopped me from being a patriot. I was born American. I was born in America. Some of my forefathers were native-American (Indians), most immigrated from other countries, yet all of them were here in the new world before the revolutionary war. Which means that from the very beginning, my people were American. I, as an American, descended from the first Americans, take great pride and identity in my lineage. I read the Declaration of Independence and the Constitution regularly. I have served in both the Army National Guard and the United States Marine Corps. My oath of enlistment was taken seriously.

"I, Michael Wilcox, do solemnly swear that I will support and defend the Constitution of the United States against all enemies foreign and domestic; that I will bear true faith and allegiance to the same; and that I will obey the orders of the President of the United States and the orders of the officers appointed over me according to regulations and the Uniform Code of Military Justice. So help me God."

To me, patriotism is a core value of being American.

When I was in the United States Marine Corps, graduating from basic training in Paris Island, South Carolina, I could not help but stand tall and proud. The sense of being a Marine, a true warrior filled my very being. Two things about that day. First, I had accomplished something that I knew the majority of Americans, and the world for that matter, would never accomplish. Second, I was officially a part of something greater then myself. That is the thing. The real thing. As men, we long to be a part of something greater then ourselves. That sense of belonging to a greater thing can drive us, inspire us, and cause us to blossom into that which we were made to be. Throughout history, when men have belonged to a brotherhood, great things have been able to happen. True, both good and bad things, but great none-the-less. However, even among those that have abused their brotherhood to accomplish something bad, the qualities of honor, loyalty, and duty were held in the highest of regards. And yet, even within the brotherhoods, some men excel to places of astonishing and inspiring acts. These men we call hero's. They become the mighty men, the men that inspire us and cause us to strive for even more. They exceed the boundaries of honor, loyalty, and duty as we know and understand them. They create a higher standard and a new height to our striving.

"America was not built on fear. America was built on courage, on imagination and an unbeatable determination to do the job at hand." - Harry Truman, President of the United States of America

I don't know if a man ever outgrows the sense of desire to be the hero. We may grow cold and calloused in some of our thoughts, but deep within us remains a flicker of love and admiration for the man that exceeds all others in heroic actions. That flicker of hope remains permanently smoldering within us, longing for us to be someones hero. We are inspired by the great orations of men throughout history that have encouraged us and gave us a sense of purpose and identity. In movies like Brave Heart, when Mel Gibson gave the speech that inspired men onward to victory against great odds, it stoked that flicker with-in the men that caused them to rally around a brotherhood and common cause. There is something naturally ingrained with-in men that says "I am a warrior." This was something endowed within us by our creator. Consequently, if it was placed within us by our creator, then it is there for a purpose.

Now, I am not speaking of some sinful nature that we are born with, that is made manifest in tendencies that we choose to let live or to master. Instead, I am speaking of something at the core of who we are. We have purpose, and that purpose demands certain qualities to exist within us. Qualities such as Honor, loyalty, and duty.

Today, things have radically changed in a wrongful attempt to not hurt anyone's feelings or offend anyone about anything. Therefore, many fine institutions that once taught qualities of honor, loyalty, and duty have become nothing more then politically correct clubs. However, even within most of them remains some of their core values.

"I tremble for my country when I reflect that God is just; that His justice cannot sleep forever." - Thomas Jefferson, 1871

When I was young, I grew up in a a scouting home. Cub Scouts, Girl Scouts, and Boy Scouts were an important part of our whole family. My parents, myself, and all of my siblings participated in the scouting organization. Our summers were spent on staff at our local scout camp. Winters consisted of hikes and weekend camping trips in snow covered mountains. Learning to build fires, construct shelters, and preform first aid were all normal lessons for us.

Some of the things that became deeply ingrained in myself and my brothers was the Boy Scout Oath, Boy Scout Law, and the Boy Scout Motto.

Boy Scout Oath: *On my honor, I will do my best. O do my duty* *to God and my country and to obey the scout law. To help other people at all times; To keep myself physically strong, mentally awake, and morally straight.*

Boy Scout Law: *A scout is trustworthy, loyal, helpful, friendly, courteous, kind, obedient, cheerful, thrifty, brave, clean, and reverent.*

Boy Scout Motto: *Always Be Prepared.*

These things helped to define who we would go on to become as men.

You could say that patriotism was bred into me and many others from the time we were little. After all I grew up in a generation of God, baseball, and mom's apple pie! We said the pledge of allegiance every morning, had a time of prayer in school, and sang the national anthem at all sporting events without trying to get creative in its delivery.

Patriotic Foundations

After I left the Marine Corps, I was active in groups and "conspiracy" meetings with other like-minded patriots. We were firm believers in the "peoples rights" and our right to govern ourselves through properly elected officials. We never trusted big government and centralized governmental power. After the Oklahoma City Bombing, the conspiracy theories gained more momentum. Unanswered questions, the official story changing, explosion patterns that didn't fit the publicized blast story, were just some of the problems. In addition to all of this was the fact that the records for Janet Reno's Bureau of Alcohol, Tobacco, and Firearms,

Waco massacre, were supposedly stored there and resulted in the destruction of significant evidence in the legality of that raid. This resulted in the establishment of the Anti-terrorism and Effective Death Penalty Act of which we saw as a direct threat upon our form of Constitutional Republic as laid out in America's Constitution. These were also the days of the "Black Helicopters". The official government story was that these unmarked, flat-black aircraft did not exist. However, myself and many others saw them on a regular basis. We would contact air traffic controllers on duty when we would spot these unmarked aircraft and they would tell us that nothing was there and there was no air traffic in that area. Latter they built a well guarded annex to our local regional airport. At the same time we noticed an increase to the "mythical" black helicopter flights in our area. Eventually, a couple of us were able to make a small reconnaissance patrol to the airport annex. What we saw amazed us. Flat black, unmarked helicopters would land on a tarmac landing field. Men in suits who "gave-off" the demeanor of C.I.A. Would get out of the aircraft that were piloted by uniformed men in black BDU's with no insignia or markings. As soon as the helicopter was shut down, other black uniformed men would wheel the aircraft into a waiting hanger and close the door. As you can imagine, this activity combined with the governments blatant denial of its existence caused quite a stir among the conspiracy crowd.

These are just a couple of examples of things that were going on that appeared to lend to the idea that there was an intentional design to alter our form of government, circumventing the rights of the people and the rights of the states. We believed that there would come a day when a nationalized police force would be created centralizing the federal governments reign over free Americans. Mind you, this was all long before the formation of the Department of Homeland Security! In those days we couldn't even imagine such an obvious federal police/militia force being accepted by the people at large. Our guess back then was that they would have the majority of our military forces deployed overseas, intentionally causing some catastrophic, civil hardship in our country and bringing United Nation troops in to act as peace-keeping forces here. We were outraged at the thought of Russian troops shooting at American citizens with our own governments blessing!

As time went on, many things occurred that gave us alarm, yet we were regarded as "paranoid", "conspiracy theorists", " right-wing extremists", "alarmists", and "war-mongers." People would listen, then chuckle and explain to us that that kind of stuff would never happen here. Meanwhile, we never stopped searching for what the real agenda was.

Among us, "conspiracy nuts" was a well know man who exposed the truth every chance he could over the short wave radio. Eventually, he was hunted down and assassinated by our government. This was right after the twin towers were brought down by Muslims bent on the destruction of America. The Twin Tower attack on September 11, 2001 changed the world forever. I am not sure that any other single event altered the future of mankind like this one single event. Obviously, the birth, crucifixion, and resurrection of Jesus surpassed even this, but I am speaking of the things of man here.

"In the first place we should insist that if the immigrant who comes here in good faith becomes and American and assimilates himself to us, he shall be treated on an exact equality as everyone else, for it is an outrage to discriminate against any such man because of creed, or birthplace, or origin. But this is predicated upon the man's becoming in very fact an American, and nothing but an American... There can be no divided allegiance here. Any man who says he is an American, but something else also, isn't an American at all. We have room for but one flag, the American flag, and this excludes the red flag, which symbolizes all wars against liberty and civilization, just as much as it excludes any foreign flag of a nation to which we are hostile...We have room but for one language here, and that is the English language...And we have room but for one sole loyalty and that is a loyalty to the American people."
- Theodore Roosevelt - President of the United States of America

Because I didn't "meet" Jesus and surrender my life to Him until April of 2004, you can imagine how September 11th affected me. The first and foremost question to us was "Why did this happen?" I'm sure everyone was asking that question, but in the conspiracy world, that question takes on much deeper meanings. As an example, it is believed by many that Hitler and his cronies staged the attack on the Reichstag building in 1933. A young communist named Marinus Van derr Lubbe was arrested, he admitted to starting the fire, and was executed over it. Hitler, being recently elected to the position of Chancellor of Germany a few weeks earlier, encouraged German President Paul Von Hindenburg to pass an emergency decree that suspended civil liberties allowing the Nazi party to consolidate control over Germany. Eventually this led to the attempt at world domination by Hitler and the Nazis.

In the months following September 11th, the whole situation began to look eerily like a Reichstag false flag situation. What we saw then, and still see today, is an increased loss of civil liberties here in America, and a centralizing and consolidating of federal authority. The establishment of The Department of Homeland Security has done nothing more then fan the flames of paranoia.

"Truth will ultimately prevail where there is pains taken to bring it to light." - George Washington, President, in a letter to Charles M. Thruston, August 10, 1794

I understand your skepticism at this point. If you are like most mainstream Americans you are probably thinking that these conspiracy nut-jobs take everything out of context.

Some do. I could never argue that. However, I like to think that as for myself, and most of the people I hung around with, we gave much consideration to our claims and beliefs. We tried as well as we could to allow the evidence as we were aware of it, to speak for itself. One thing that has remained true since history began, is that a strong few will always try to dominate the majority for their own glory and power. With few exceptions throughout history, power corrupts most people and organizations.

"The strongest reason for the people to retain the right to keep and bear arms is, as a last resort, to protect themselves against tyranny in government." - Thomas Jefferson

The Department of Homeland Security is truly the largest threat to ever come against the civil liberties and Constitutional rights of Americans. They are a larger threat then radical Islam and terrorism because they come disguised as our friend here to protect us. An army is always a threat to the people. However, it is a necessary entity in the defense of a people. The American military might is governed by a strict set of boundaries that prohibits them, for the most part, from operating domestically, and in specific, against American citizens. For the military might of the United States to be deployed, it takes an act of Congress. This means that many elected Congressmen and Senators must agree that our military is needed. It is actually a little more complicated then that. First we had Posse Comitatus act of 1878 under President Hayes. Basically it limits the power of the federal government to use federal military forces to enforce domestic polices. Unfortunately, the department of the Navy, which includes the Marine Corps, is not mentioned in the act. Technically they could be used in an enforcement fashion. However, their rules subjugate them to adhere to it more out of courtesy then requirement. Until 2001, the Posse Comitatus Act kept the people safe from the government forcing the people against their will into a form of government that "we the people" did not duly vote for. On October 26, 2001, forty-five days after the attack on the twin towers in New York City, President Bush signed into law the U.S.A. P.A.T.R.I.O.T Act. It is actually an acronym for "Uniting and Strengthening America by Providing Appropriate Tools Required to Intercept and Obstruct Terrorism Act of 2001."

This Act effectively modifies the 4th Amendment rights of the people regarding search and seizure. Under the Patriot Act, the government no longer needs an order signed by a judge to gain access to your personal information. Basically, with a National Security Letter (NSL) issued by FBI agents without a judges approval (which gives no oversight or accountability) the government may collect your personal information such as: banking records, phone records, computer records, and your credit history.

"My reading of history convinces me that most bad government results from too much government." - Thomas Jefferson

The 4th Amendment of our Constitution was added by our founding fathers to protect the citizens of this Republic from unjust practices from a government that disenfranchises the very people they are to govern. The framers of our Constitution understood all to clearly the injustices of government that forgot its purpose. We can establish that by the general frame-work of our constitution and these words in our Deceleration of Independence - "Governments are instituted among men, deriving their just powers from the consent of the governed."

"Necessity is the plea of every infringement of human freedom. It is the argument of tyrants and the creed of slaves." - *William Pitt, the younger 1783*

On this tack of discussion I could go on and on, but I think you are beginning to see my point. Laws and our government are changing and eroding our basic freedoms and liberties guaranteed to us under our constitution.

For the interested, of which all Americans should be, there is a plethora of reliable information about the changing of our laws that violate and infringe upon our rights as a free people.

Allow me to get back to the threat of an organization like the Department of Homeland Security. Most people really do not know the scope of authority that the Department of Homeland Security holds. The Washington Post did a 2 year investigative study into the Department of Homeland Security and what they uncovered should frighten most people in the world today. Nobody knows for certain how many employees it has, how many departments it has, what all the departments do, how much money it spends or has in its budget. Below are just a few of the investigations findings:

> Some 1,271 government organizations and 1,931 private companies work on programs related to counter-

terrorism, homeland security, and intelligence in some 10,000 locations across the United States.

> An estimated 854,000 people hold top secret security clearances (through DHS)

> Only a handful of senior officials from the Defense Department are even allowed to know what goes on in DHS.

> There are 51 federal and military command centers operating in 15 Major cities across the United States that monitor and track finances.

Understand this, The Department of Homeland Security is the third largest organization on the Presidents cabinet. It is only superseded by the Department of Defense and the Department of Veterans Affairs.

To follow is a list (not comprehensive) of the areas DHS controls:

- U.S. Citizen and Immigration Services
- U.S. Customs and Boarder Protection
- U.S. Immigration and Customs Enforcement
- Transportation Security Administration
- U.S. Coast Guard
- United States Secret Service
- Federal Emergency Management Agency

"Power, like a desolating pestilence, pollutes whate'er it touches, and obedience, bane of all genius, virtue, freedom, truth, makes slaves of men, and of the human frame, a mechanized automation." - Percy Byesshe Shelley

The Department of Homeland Security is predicted to receive control of state and local law enforcement. Our current sitting President Barrack Obama is pushing very hard to nationalize our law enforcement. This will take it out of the control of the people and place it in the hands of a centralized government. Some may not really understand the dangers of such an action. However, they are real. The more centralized the governmental control, the less individuality we are allowed to retain as a people. This includes, political viewpoints, philosophies and philosophical ideas, religious beliefs, child rearing practices, educational options, recreational activities, life-style practices; the list can go on for a very long time. In fact, we, in many ways, already see the fore-shadowing of a completely changed landscape here in America. We currently have the most divisive government in America's 240 year history. The current policies of the Obama administration are succeeding in dividing the American people in every opportunistic forum. Race, politics, religion, economics, nationality, and the list goes on. As examples, "The Black Lives Matter" movement. Never condemned by our federal government even though they expressly call for the killing of law enforcement and white Americans. The United States Attorney General announcing that any {American} using language that could be construed as inciting violence against Muslims would be prosecuted to the fullest ability of her office. Even going so far as to have legislation proposed before congress making it a law protecting Islam while excluding all other religions. The overstepping of Constitutional authority by the current Supreme Court in creating a law forcing gay and lesbian agendas. The United States Supreme Court, by United States Constitution, has no authority to create legislation, but rather to rule upon the constitutionality of legislative actions. In other words, Congress and the Senate make law, the U.S. Supreme Court determine if such law is constitutional.

The Nazi party was restricted by the technology of their era. The technology in place today is frightful to say the least.

The problem with consolidated government in a republic such as ours, is the vanquishing of individuality. You see, we are the United States of America. We are 50 sovereign governing states, ruled through an electoral process of representation, united under a centralized federal government established by constitution to deal with interstate and international relations. If we remove the sovereignty of the states, you must also remove the individuality of the people. Our form of government is unlike anything else in the world. Sadly, once we are consolidated we will be just like every other country. The goal of which is for eventual unification of all nations under one form of international government.

The plea of necessity, that eternal argument of all conspirators." - William Henry Harrison, 1829

Did you know there is an agenda to reduce the worlds population? You can't even make this stuff up. I am serious. According to the powers to be in the global scheme, the ideal population of planet Earth is 500 million people. Considering there are nearly 7 billion people on the planet, that means 6.5 billion people have to go. Currently they estimate that the world population will be around 10 billion by 2050+/-. A more liberal optimum global population is set at between 1.5 billion and 2 billion people in a Stanford

News article from July 11, 1994. From the World Watch Institute " *That there will be a large-scale reduction in global human numbers over the next two or three centuries appears to be inevitable. The primary issue seems to be whether this process will be under conscious human control and (hopefully) relatively benign, or whether it will turn out to be unpredictably chaotic and (perhaps) catastrophic. We must begin our new manner of thinking about this critically important global issue now, so that Einstein's prescient and legitimate concerns about human and civilizational survival into the 21ˢᵗ century and beyond may be addressed as rapidly, fully, and humanely as possible.*"

Listen, this is not just a few quack's from the fringe that believe this and feel as though this is a pressing issue that must be dealt with now. At the Yale School of Forestry and Environmental Studies, The World Watch organization, Professors at Stanford University, Professors at the University of Texas at Austin, Ted Turner (founder of C.N.N.), Mikhail Gorbachev (former President of The Soviet Union), The director of the Earth Institute at Columbia University (Jeffery D. Sachs), and the list goes on. This issue is believed to be so serious that the United Nations has taken to address it on multiple levels. The framework was laid in it's "Agenda 21". The United nations Women – a United Nations entity for for gender equality and the empowerment of women is pushing for global abortion on demand, more sterilization programs, massive forced government interference in family life to curb population growth (the New American Thursday, October 30, 2014). The United Nations also openly recommends the redistribution of child rearing responsibilities from the family to the state (government). Often, when speaking or writing publicly, global population concerns are hidden among a wide range of global topics typically referred to as "{Global, World, etc.} Sustainable Development" This includes pollution, global warming, population growth and location/relocation, resource consumption and availability, and so many other things that concern mankind in general.

"Fear is what is needed in despotism. Virtue is not at all necessary, and honor would be dangerous." - Charles-Louis de Secondat, Baron de Montesquieu, 1748

In a book on American patriotism and Christianity, you may be wondering what relevance all this has with this books topic. I can understand your concern and it is a good question. Our current president, and several previous presidents support the policies and agendas of the United Nations. President Bush's constant phrase of the New World Order was based on United Nations policies and concerns. Basically, their agenda is quickly becoming our agenda. We, America, are leading by example in the realm of implementing sustainable global policies. These policies allow a foreign entity (The United Nations) to dictate American policy; whose membership widely believes that the Constitution of the United States is an outdated document and is no longer relevant to today's world. On September 25, 2014, in President Obama's address to the United Nations, he outlined several strategies to improve relationships with all countries on the planet. Even going as far as implying that the United States Constitution is outdated and needs to be revised for the changing times. The overall thinking of educational systems and world leaders is that we must merge governments so as to be similar in structure allowing international law and policies to determine our course. This way is completely contrary to the notion of sovereignty. Because they not only think this way, but wholeheartedly believe it, that means for it to come to fruition, there must be a concerted, intentional means to implement these policies. This means that America as we know it must be changed. Whether by force or by benign means or a blending of both.

"The tree of liberty must be refreshed from time to time with the blood of patriots and tyrants." - Thomas Jefferson

The Constitution of The United States established a foundation for this country. We declared, through the writing and deliverance of the Deceleration of Independence, the ratification of the Constitution of the United States, the blood shed by so many new American citizens, and the first elections of our new government, that we were a sovereign country. We were a Judaeo - Christian country. Not that all of our founding fathers were Christian. Only that the framework of our government and laws were laid upon Judaeo – Christianity and not some other religious foundation such as Islam. By and large, America was a Christian country since almost all of here citizenry either were Christians or believed in the Christian God. We were not formed as a theocracy, meaning that we are not a religious government. We would no longer be forced by the church, through the government, to adhere to a certain set of standards and life. We believed that in our new Republic, we the people would govern ourselves through elected officials by the people. However, at the same time, we were (by overwhelming majority) still Christians.

Our founding fathers also established some foundational principals that echo throughout the halls of our being as Americans and Patriots.

- "We hold these truths to be self evident, that all men are created equal, that they are endowed by their creator with certain unalienable rights, that among these are life, liberty, and the pursuit of happiness. --That to secure these rights, Governments are instituted among men, deriving their just powers from the consent of the governed, --That whenever any form of government becomes destructive towards these ends, it is the right of the people to alter or abolish it, and to institute new government, laying its foundation on such principals and organizing its powers in such form as to them shall seem most likely to effect their safety and happiness."
- That no religion should be forced upon the people by the government.
- That men should not live in fear of their government.
- That men, when accused have a right to face their accuser and to have a fair and just trial.
- That powers not explicitly given to the federal government by the constitution should be reserved for the state governments.
- And finally, in a guarantee to maintain the right of the people to be free from a tyrannical government, the right of men to maintain weapons

was believed to be important enough to be included as one of the first constitutional laws for men of this country.

All of these foundations can be found in the illustrated context, in our Declaration of Independence and our federal Constitution.

"No man ever ruled other men for their own good...no man ever ruled other men for anything except for their undoing." - George D. Herron, 1920

Today we find ourselves as Americans, living in a nation that increasingly ignores the will of the people at large; filled with corrupt, life-long politicians, who have lost touch with the very people they were elected to govern. To become president requires an unimaginable sum of money for the majority of all Americans. Many new laws are being created through a loop-hole known as "Executive Orders" created to allow the office of president to create legally binding orders to help officers and agencies of the executive branch to manage operations within the federal government itself. These Executive Orders carry the full weight and authority of law when they take authority from a legislative power which grants its power directly to the Executive (Executive Office) by the Constitution, or are made pursuant to Acts of Congress that explicitly delegate to the President some degree of discretionary power. Most of these laws circumvent the will of the people and the intent of our forefathers in the creation of laws. Although an Executive Order can (and should be) reviewed by judicial review, they seldom are. Throughout the history of the United States we have never seen such use of this Executive privilege as we have seen in the last few presidents since its peak during the days of president Franklin D. Roosevelt. However,we have never seen such gross and blatant disregard for the voice of the people or legislative process as we have seen in our current president Barrack H. Obama. Throughout presidency's there have often been very unpopular and controversial policies that have been introduced and implemented. None, however, have shaken the foundation of civil liberties and our deeply held constitutional beliefs as what has been going on in the times since President Ronald Reagan. President Reagan, and I realize this point is nothing more then my personal opinion, was the last great American president that we have had. I would not call myself truly Republican or Democrat, just an American. I admire both Bush's, more-so the second President Bush. Unfortunately, even with their apparent love for America, they really pushed for changes that violate our sovereignty and move us into the New World Order, globalizing our policies to sustain a world cooperative thus compromising national sovereignty.

"The accumulation of all power, legislative, executive, and judiciary, in the same hands, whether of one, a few, or many, and whether hereditary, self-appointed, or elective, may justly be pronounced the very definition of tyranny." - James Madison, 1788

There is so much going on and its pace seems to be quickening. We no longer have privacy, everything we do is subject to being watched and monitored by our own government. The very people entrusted to safeguard us. Senior military officials are being forced out of service because they object to policies that are unconstitutional or questionable. Drones used against U.S. Citizens, NSA and other intelligence gathering breaching laws with no repercussions to the guilty. Americans being abducted by our own government, by-passing proper jurisprudence and being held in undisclosed locations for up to a year. Our own government has become the bully on the school yard. As if all of that is not enough, the media has become puppets of the government. They tote party lines and generally only object to government policy enough to say that they are being objective, but when it comes right down to it they don't want to risk alienating themselves from the government press conferences. In addition to that, they use fear as a great tool to sell agendas and politics. Every story reported is twisted to suit whatever is being promoted by the president. Whenever you have any news organization that even attempts to be objective in their reporting they are ridiculed and glossed over. Today, Americans live in perpetual fear. They need now more then ever, heroic Americans to look up too. Today we live in an era in which the future sovereignty of our great nation will remain or forever be lost.

"I have sworn upon the alter of God eternal hostility against every form of tyranny over the mind of men."
Thomas Jefferson, 3ʳᵈ U.S. President
Founding Father

"I'm proud to be an American, where at least I know I'm free..."
...but, what does the Bible say about patriotism, honor, loyalty, and duty?

...Actually, quite a bit.

America is changing, there is absolutely no doubt about that. Anyone who has watched President Barrack Obama's last State of the Union address could hear the overtones of a global order and the unification of the world. He is not alone, these overtones and globalizing "talk" can be heard from congressmen and woman, political candidates, educational leaders, and international leaders. Increasingly, there is a global "force of influence" that is bringing about change in the values and policies of the United States of America.

To some, what I am about to say next may sound like the splitting of hairs, but it is an important point to differentiate in. America was not founded as a Christian country. It was a country founded upon Christian values and ideologies. If we were founded as a Christian government, then Christianity would be our national religion and in the most extreme sense, all citizens would then be required to be Christian. This is not the case for America. America is not a theocracy. America is a Republic established upon the values and beliefs of Christianity. Our laws and policies were clearly established upon the teachings of Christ and His church. This was in the beginning of our great Republic. Today, it is quite obvious that our Republic's values, and therefore the citizens whose voices are clearly heard, is separating from our founding values. From examples of Roe vs. Wade, to educational mandates, current rulings from the Supreme Court, to financial support for government supported programming. This list grows and becomes to cumbersome to list in any detail here. We, as Christians, can point fingers in all kinds of directions that we want to. However, before we make accusations, allow us to first look in the mirror. It is our fault that these changes do and have occurred.

The Indictment

"...How so?" You may ask. Simple. As a form of government that is founded upon the basic principals and ideologies of Christianity, it becomes the responsibility of Christianity to safeguard the foundations of such government. When Christianity fails to safeguard these foundations, another ideology shall, without fail, move to bring about change in the foundational ideologies of such government. Whether these outside ideologies should be from the self promoting wisdom of humanism or some other religious philosophy. These foreign concepts of order and law will undoubtedly move to establish themselves as the rightful masters of thought. Furthermore, it is not the task of those who are not followers of Christian values to safeguard the foundational principals of our Republic. They are not bound by the laws of God in the way that we who are the Church are. Some have a compromised or warped understanding of Christianity. Some are bound by the deception of false beliefs, while others, blinded by their own sense of self importance, deny God altogether, building instead upon the foundation of Humanism.

It is the Church that has long sat quiet and complacent in the comforts of our great republic. We have endured the undercutting of Christian values in our society, not out of an endurance born of patience and kindness, but rather the form of endurance that is born from complacent human tolerance. We, as the Church, would rather suffer that which is short-sited in its wisdom and is therefore complacent in its comfort, yielding instead to human desire then to a righteous charge before God. When we find ourselves on the verge of utter destruction of that which we had charge over, we cry foul! We as men given to our lowly human desires, choose to lay the blame for our own thriftless stewardship at the foot of another instead of taking the responsibility of our our own failure at steadfast devotion to safeguard the foundation of our great republic.

It is because of this apathy in the burden of responsibility in protecting the very foundational intent of our forefathers of this republic that we find ourselves today in a country we barely recognize and have become a marginalized voice among the people this great land.

We, the Church of the glorious Savior of mankind, have utterly failed in the trust granted to us for the preservation of a way of life that is a heritage to be passed from one generation to the next. In this, my fellow Christ followers, we who are also Americans, have not only failed our sons and our daughters, we have failed the world. For America, as a sovereign nation, independent of the rule of others, shone as a light of great hope among all men. It was the foundational ideologies of America that demonstrated to all humankind throughout the globe, that the chains of oppression could be shattered and the light of deliverance from such oppression could be seen in the darkest of nations. We heralded freedom, and hope, and equality to all men. Not through the endeavors of humanistic self sufficiency, but through the hope that is found only in Jesus the Christ. We, the American church, have betrayed the Church of Christ in this.

It is true that we may be able to point to so many accomplishments in the advancement of the Kingdom of God throughout our history as a sovereign nation. For it is the American church that leads the way in funding for Christian Kingdom enlargement. It is from the purse of the American church that pours out with an incomparable generosity for this very purpose. It is the American church that publishes more written literature to teach and grow Christian faith throughout the world. It is the American church that has become the economic building block of Christ's Church around the world. In addition, the world has seen humanitarian aid delivered to all men and nations from the wealth of America which was motivated by the foundational values derived from Christ's Church in America. Yet all these things are considered but a temporary success when the very instrument that allows these glorious works of God's people to be seen throughout the world are unguarded and allowed to fall into ruin. We, the Church in America have failed the world when we forsake such important trust which has been honored upon us by God in Heaven.

The question therefore, begs to be asked, "Is it too late to restore our nation?"

In short, the answer is yes it is too late for that. No, that is not the answer I want to hear and it probably not the answer you want to hear either. At best we can delay the inevitable. The complexity of the reasons for this would require far more space then I have committed to for this brief booklet. However, each of you is free to examine in further depth the various possible avenues to restore our great nation to its former glory. Unfortunately, I am confident that you will also arrive at the same conclusion as I have in this matter. In this booklet I will try to briefly address the highlights of why we cannot restore our great republic to its first form.

The hopeless cure.

There are several avenues to bring about the change needed. First, for the Church, it requires us to recognize our failure. Followed quickly by repentance. Not just the collection of mighty words strung together and the beating of ones chest; bowing ones head for a day in humility. Instead, it would require a genuine heart change for the American church at large. It would require a true humbling of the people of Christ here in America. A unity of determination and scheme. With the distinctive diversity found in today's church, this by itself is a doubtful thing to happen of our own effort. It would take a force of circumstances greater then our diversity to drive us together in this common purpose. Although I have stated with great confidence that we will never resurrect this republic of the people to its former greatness and godliness, all is not lost in this first need. If this nearly insurmountable goal were to be conquered in this day by the church, then a glimmer of hope remains for this nation to again be a nation established on Christian principal and philosophy. Yet, if the church does not attain such daunting union within itself, the circumstances on the horizon are such that the church will be driven to such unity for the common purpose of survival. In that common purpose of survival we may not see our great country rise to it's former godly nature, but we will surely see the glory of God made manifest among His people. For the true and undeniable power of Christ's Church is always made visible in the harshest of persecutions. Therefore, in the respect of the Church here in America, it will simply transform from the subtle beauty it once was to the brilliant polish that is always brought about in the persecution of the Saints. However, for our nation, when the brilliance of the Church in America is made visible, the nation will have exchanged it's godly attire for the rags of men, and the America known by our fathers will have perished.

The first course for all American patriots is simple on the surface, yet nearly impossible in it's implementation. That is our process of election. The problem is not just our executive, but also our legislative. Both must be radically changed. In the Congress and Senate we have a population of elected officials who speak from both sides of their head and covet their power more then the people they represent. True there may be a small few who are the exception to this, but the reality is that most are career politicians who are disconnected from their constituency. Increasingly they are more unified with the interests of the "global thinking" of the current world then of the sovereignty of our nation. You cannot replace just a few legislators. All must go. Not only do they need replaced with fresh blood from the people, but they must be a people who see the enemy of sovereignty that is the global order. The interests of the nation must outweigh the interests of the global community, or the individuality of the nation will be lost. Not only this, but those new blood citizens must also hold sacred the foundational concepts found in our Constitution and Bill of Rights. The intention of the framework of our Constitutional Republic must be an uncompromising statute among our elected officials. They must be zealous for the preservation of our nation as laid before us in these documents.

Now, if the Congress and the Senate were overthrown by electoral process, with members of such patriotic integrity as I have aforementioned, then we could, within a single generation, see our nation once again restored to its former self. Even if our executive were as it is today, yet our legislative, by force of action and resolve, treasured the sacred and honorable responsibility of their office beyond all other forces and influence, then our nation would again shine with it's former glory.

If we elect to the executive, a man filled with honor and patriotism for our nation, he will find his every intention thwarted by the power of the legislative that remains as it is today. Both Congress and the less mentioned Senate are more loyal to their political parties and the special interests that line their pockets, and the pockets of their parties, then their sacred responsibilities as the elected voice of the people. With an honorable man in the executive, the corrupt traitors of the legislative would solidify in a hardened front against the executive. At the best he will find that his good intentions have become nothing more then compromised policies and hollow promises.

With the office of President as the face of America, we often forget that all three branches of our government must work together to bring about change. There is little we can do in the Judicial Branch as they are appointed. However, should we resolve the tyranny that has infested the executive and the legislative; the judicial would also be sorted.

The second course of action for American patriots is one that should be reserved for the action of last resort. That is the forced eviction of the traitors to our Constitutional Republic. In this course of action, the situation would, in all likelihood, quickly escalate to armed insurrection. This in itself has an outcome that is doubtful to the interests of the American patriot. We would have to have the military, or at least a sizable portion of the military allied to such patriotic endeavor. Even with the might of the military behind the American patriot, a bloody fight would surely ensue. The Department of Homeland Security is an army unto its own, and that army is controlled directly by the executive. This course of action is really the only viable course left to the true American today. Unfortunately, even should the Americans who are loyal to America find the resolve to initiate such a necessary extermination of treason of the highest offices of our government, it would cause such a shaking in the fabric of the global order that, in all likelihood, it would initiate another world war. I do not say this to deter faithful Americans from this action, but that the weight of such radical cleansing of tyrannical agents would be assessed before setting ourselves to such commitment.

Unfortunately, unless some less globally impacting, and less savage undertaking can be brought about to reclaim our rightful government that is For the People and By the

People, we would be left with no choice. The day, if not upon us already, is quickly coming in which the sovereignty of our great nation will be extinguished in all but name. And in that day, the true American, the one that holds the sovereignty of our Constitutional Republic, The United States of America, to be of paramount importance to himself and to the world, would be faced with willingness to stand and fight, or to surrender in disgrace and failure.

This very thing has brought me finally to the reason for the writing of this booklet. What is the place of the Christian in America today? Can we remain a patriot in the truest sense without conflict to our citizenship in a higher kingdom, or must we face a choice between American Patriotism and Christianity?

To answer this, we must first examine our charge from our beloved Savior and see if the two ideologies come to a clashing or can continue to run in parallel.

The Kingdom Minded Follower

It is a well known fact that we could walk through scripture and cause it to justify almost any predetermined position. I could pile scripture upon scripture on my justifying argument, demonstrating how the Israelite's were commanded by God for the defense of their nation. I can justify violence and hate, and prejudice. I can justify practically any position I choose to take in this argument. There are so many deceivers out there today that somewhere today, someone is claiming that Christians are justified in violence. We have teachers of false doctrine right now, some with big names and tens of thousands of followers that twist scripture on a regular basis. They teach the "Healthy, wealthy, easy – living, God wants you to have no problems gospel." Which is no gospel at all. They spout off sermon after sermon. Selling book after book. Videos, mega-church live-streaming, high dollar conferences, and through it all; they pour out scripture to defend their argument. Never mind that it violates the continuity of Jesus's teachings in general, let alone the continuity of the Word of God entirely. Forget the fact that history proves otherwise. Ignore the the hungry, the sick, and the suffering all over the world who are absolutely sold out for Jesus and His cause. Pretend that they do not exist or that their complete surrender to Christ is somehow less then ours here in the American church. No, it is better that we cater to the flesh, disguising it as spiritual enlightenment. Who needs the real face of Christian endurance when we can feel good, have a windfall of blessings from heaven that translate into creature comforts, financial prosperity, and healthful well-being.   ...No, this is not Kingdom mindedness. This is not what it means to follow Jesus. Those teachings are not what it means to be blessed of the Lord. It does not matter how elegantly I speak. How uplifting my words are. It does not make it a right belief and a holy principal because "I have made millions and you can too." That is a wickedness that exceeds the evil perpetrated by those who do not claim Jesus! These false teachers are worse then Nero when he burned the saints alive as if they were candles to light his lavish banquets.

Kingdom mindedness is to set the way of Christ's kingdom ahead of ourselves and our own desires. A good place to start is in the Gospel of Matthew. Here was the way of Jesus written by one who walked with the Son of God when He was in the form of man. He witnessed the words from Jesus's very mouth and later wrote them down so that they would benefit those of us who came after.

When we look at chapter 5 of the Gospel of Matthew we find the beginning of what we refer to as the Sermon on the mount. This is probably one of the most comprehensive recorded teachings that flowed from Jesus's very lips on His expectations for those who follow Him.

When we examine the Gospel and the letters {Epistles} written by John, we capture the heart of a kingdom man. A true follower of Jesus and what that looks like. Here was a man that sat under Jesus teaching as one of the original followers. He lived a long life, as many as 80 years after first meeting Jesus. He lived the life he proclaimed; he walked out what he was taught. He taught a single-minded loyalty to Christ. Even if that single-minded loyalty cost everything we have, even our life.

Read the letters of Paul. Here we have a man who was radically transformed by Christ. He brings us a depth of understanding to God's Holy Word that enables us to move past legalism and into a heart transformation. He suffered unimaginable hardships, and yet it did nothing more then solidify his allegiance to Christ and harden his stance as a true kingdom man.

Through Luke, who is considered to be a first rate historian, we can see a record of the early church. We can see what the first believers were motivated by. We can understand their dedication and commitment to the way of Christ.

Starting from the Old Testament and traveling through the New Testament, we see a continuity of motive and discipline. When thought or teaching violate this, then it is false. It makes no difference how many passages of scripture one can use to defend their argument. If the teaching does not travel along the lines of scriptural continuity, then it is a false understanding of scripture. Furthermore, when we examine from the Old to the New, we can see a progression of spiritual maturity. Starting with Adam we find very basic and simple law. With Abraham, we find specific law that is physical in form and discipline yet benefits man eternally. With Jesus we find the realization of the inability of mankind to be saved by the adherence to the law and grace appears. Through grace we find the revelation that legality is not nullified, but instead, it becomes fulfilled. The road of grace, that path of Jesus, the following of His way, creates a heart change and out of this changed heart flows the natural adherence to law.

Much like the progression of the infant who learns the basic laws of "no" and "yes." They progress into the years of toddler-ship where the laws are to become "engraved in stone." As parents we demand obedience from our child. As they approach and enter into the teenage years, and then into the early adult years, we begin to focus less on the legality of the law and more on the heart of the individual. As the heart is transformed into a mature young adult, the fulfillment of the law becomes a natural byproduct. So too is mankind's walk God.

I take the time to illustrate this point of progression and maturity so that you will understand what I am about to say next. You see, as I have pondered the place of the Christian who is an American, and who is a patriot in America (as if American and patriot should ever be separate), I have sought out the advice and counsel of many men who have walked this walk of faith far longer then myself. What I found was that the thoughts of these men are greatly divided. Not only is this a subject which troubles me, but it is a subject that is divided among the American church at large.

I read through the Word of God, pray before God, and meditate on scripture, seeking to unravel this difficult position for myself and so many others. The sacredness of the Constitution of the United States and it's Bill of Rights is something held closely to the hearts of many Americans in the church. Especially to those who have served in the armed forces and those who have taken an oath to defend it. In the past, there has been little reason to even consider that these two ideologies could clash. In the most general sense, America was a Christian nation, with Christian values, and Christian admiration. Today is different. Christianity, especially right Christianity, is becoming less popular. We find that on nearly every front Christianity is being side-lined in American society. We are living in a day when we are witnessing the groundwork being laid for violent Christian persecution. In many situations we find Christians and entire church congregations rising up in protest and action out of rebellion. Sadly, this is wrong. Any action undertaken by a rebellious spirit is wrong Christianity. All Christian action must be an out-flowing of Christ-like heart and godly order. We see many prayer groups being formed to pray for our nation and this is good, but in most cases lacking. Prayer undertaken without the applicable action is like what God speaks through the prophet Isaiah:

> *"Shout it aloud, do not hold back.*
> *Raise your voice like a trumpet.*
> *Declare to my people their rebellion*
> *and to the descendants of Jacob their sins.*
> *For day after day they seek me out;*
> *they seem eager to know my ways,*

> *as if they were a nation that does what is right*
> *and has not forsaken the commands of its God.*
> *They ask me for just decisions*
> *and seem eager for God to come near to them.*
> *'Why have we fasted,' they say,*
> *'and you have not seen it?*
> *Why have we humbled ourselves,*
> *and you have not noticed?'*
> *Yet on the day of your fasting, you do as you please*
> *and exploit all your workers.*
> *Your fasting ends in quarreling and strife,*
> *and in striking each other in wicked fists.*
> *You cannot fast as you do today*
> *and expect your voice to be heard on high.*
> *Is this the kind of fast I have chosen,*
> *only a day for people to humble themselves?*
> *Is it only for bowing one's head like a reed*
> *and for lying on sack-cloth and ashes?*
> *Is this what you call a fast,*
> *a day acceptable to the Lord?"*
> Isaiah 58:1-5 (N.I.V.)

As we continue to read on in this passage we find that God is bringing a charge against the people of Israel. Yet in general, it is a charge that still holds true against His people here in America. Like the Israelite's of that day, God is calling the American Church to not just pray, but to live a life in accordance with His heart. Jesus really makes this point in the opening lines of the sermon on the mount when He says:

> *"Blessed are the poor in spirit,*
> *for theirs is the kingdom of heaven.*

Blessed are those who morn,
for they will be comforted.
Blessed are the meek,
for they will inherit the Earth.
Blessed are those who hunger and thirst for righteousness,
for they will be filled.
Blessed are the merciful,
for they will be shown mercy.
Blessed are the pure in heart,
for they will see God.
Blessed are the peacemakers,
for they will be called children of God.
Blessed are those who are persecuted because of
righteousness,
for theirs is the kingdom of heaven.
Blessed are you when people insult you, persecute you and
falsely say all kinds of evil against you because of me.
Rejoice and be glad, because great is your reward in
heaven, for in the same way they persecuted the prophets
who were before you. "
Matthew 5:3-11 (N.I.V.)

Jesus goes on in this teaching to demonstrate that when the law is fulfilled, we find ourselves still falling short of His way. Yet, when the heart is transformed to His way, the law is naturally fulfilled. That is who we are called to be. A people whose hearts are transformed to the image of God. In this way His kingdom is released upon the Earth.

This is important because it defines who we are to be. We are to be a people who release the kingdom of God upon the Earth. When we willingly submit ourselves to Jesus, we become citizens of His kingdom. We willingly follow His way, seeking out His purpose, and strive to allow His purpose to be our purpose.

This means that we are not Americans who are Christians. We are instead, Christians who are also Americans. Our first loyalty must be to God and His desire, His kingdom. We cannot have duel citizenship that both remain master. True, as Christians who live here in America, we are duel citizens. This is true for Christians who reside anywhere. They are citizens of the kingdom of God and citizens of the nation in which they are residents – their kingdom of men. This means they have citizen responsibilities to their kingdom of men – their nation, and responsibilities to the kingdom of God. So long as these responsibilities do not clash, then there is no problem and both can be adhered to in good conscious. When they clash, one must be chosen as the superior. To choose America as superior to the kingdom of God is to renounce Jesus as your Lord! To accept Jesus as your savior and Lord is to submit yourself to His authority. You willingly give Him the place of supreme authority in your life in all things. You as a man may not like or want a certain thing, but submission comes at this point. The submitted man willingly chooses God's way above his own way.

Here is the thing, so long as we try to equate American patriotism with Christianity, we have a compromised, and therefore, false theology. People will come to me with all kinds of specific examples of Patriotic Christianity, and yet it always comes back to the same place when set beside the Holy Word of God. One can maintain patriotism only for as long as the actions and values do not collide. Upon collision, a choice must be consciously made as to which authority will reign in our lives. Lip-service is not enough.

Our actions upon decision speak the real truth about our priorities in life.

The Christian in America has a sacred and honorable responsibility to vote in good conscious for our political candidates. Run for office if you so desire, but maintain your integrity before Christ. Remain uncompromised while serving out our civic duties. Be involved in local, state, and federal government. In this way what is right and just before God will persevere within our nation. Pray for our leaders, pray for our citizens. Pray for our families. Do all that can be done before God to maintain our great nation. However, when the day comes that insurrection is the only alternative left before us to maintain this great republic as it was first given to us by our fathers; then we must take stock of who we are.

> *"...render therefore unto Caesar the things which are Caesar's; and unto God the things that are God's."*
> Matthew 22:21 (K.J.V.)

This nation and it's sovereignty belongs to the Caesar's of this day, but the souls of men belong to God. Because of this, we have a Holy responsibility to advance the kingdom of God unto all men, even the men of our own nation. If I pick up arms, or support such cause against men; such men will be denied another moment to surrender their life unto God. I will become the very instrument that deprives them of the very reason that Christ hung on Calvary. I will have become the obstacle, the stumbling block, upon their very road to salvation. I will have found myself working against the cause of Christ and not for it. For I am not commissioned to be the instrument of His wrath, but instead the instrument of His mercy. I am to be a light in the darkness; a symbol of the hope that is found in Christ and in Him alone.

My garments cannot be the Red, White, and Blue; instead it must be the righteousness of God. So long as good citizenry is aligned with the precepts of God, then I shall be the best of citizen, glorifying the one true God in the conduct of an American. However, when that day comes, as it is swiftly sweeping down upon us, that it becomes unpopular as a citizen, if not even illegal, to stand as a true follower of Christ; then I shall stand unwavering and steadfast as a symbol of the hope that is found only through Christ. For it is better that I should endure all hardship, all suffrage, all neglect, and every manner of shame in my striving for men, whether friend or foe, to enter into the kingdom of God.

My citizen responsibility as an American Patriot is to support and defend the Constitution of the United States of America, and her citizens within it. My kingdom responsibility is to support and defend the cause of Christ according to His way. Our citizenship of His kingdom is separated by an eternal distance from the citizen responsibilities of the American Patriot. Therefore, as tensions mount, and the values of the Constitution of the United States of America are laid to waste in the emergence of the global community, and as the only avenue for the preservation of this great Constitutional Republic becomes increasingly a need for acts of violence; I, as a submitter to the way of Christ, must give ground to my patriotism for a nation, rendering it unto Caesar, and render my allegiance wholly unto the most hallowed of ambitions. It is the charge of Christ to illustrate His hope before all men. If I be in prison, then glorify His name before men. If I be hunted, then I must take up courage and glorify His name. If I be considered a rebel and a traitor, then I must also glorify His name.

As the Apostle to the gentiles writes:

"For our struggle is not against flesh and blood, but against the rulers, against the authorities, against the powers of this dark world and against the spiritual forces of evil in the heavenly realms."
Ephesians 6:12 (N.I.V.)

I would say, in the respect of the American Patriot and Christianity; so long as the day permits, be heard. Lobby, vote, demand change. Promote justice and constitutional law. Demand that the servants of the state act in accordance with all that is right and true and just. Stand opposed to the "global speak". Do not give into the lies of global stewardship and unified cause through-out the global community. Mankind in general stands opposed to his own creator and we, the elect of Christ, are to be His voice of hope among all men. Do not trust large centralized government and the ambitions of the corrupt and tyrannical that now dominate our governmental leadership.

However, when that day comes, and it is coming swiftly, that we cannot continue to hold the staff of "Old Glory" in one hand and the cross of Christ in the other, then set down the staff of "Old Glory" and cling wholeheartedly to the cross of Christ. For while the cause of America is just and right, it brings only a fleeting hope, and a temporary sanctuary to men, but the cause of Christ brings an eternal hope to all men. Do not hang your head low on this day of choosing, rather stand tall for now the true battle for Christ will be seen in our own land and the persecutions of the Church that will ensue, shall bring great glory to the name of Jesus, and all men around the world will see the greatness God has bestowed upon His Church. Therefore, gird up your resolve and rejoice, for the day is coming when we will be found worthy to suffer the same sufferings as our dear Lord did. Prepare the way with praising and worship to our Holy God, and encourage one another.

In conclusion

The values and traditions of America are very dear to me as they are to so many Christians I am privileged to meet here in America. Many I know have served in the armed forces, and still do today. They are strong men and women of faith and firm in their resolve that the precepts as established in the Constitution of the United States of America and our protections as citizens which are guaranteed in our Bill of rights are of supreme importance. In the terms of men, we have all believed that the United States of America is the hope of civilizations and establishes a form of government that is right and just for all men. Ensuring equality and basic human decencies. Over the years I have watched as so many of these valued treasures of the American way have been whittled away. I have watched as the threat has grown in the shadows, and cried out in warning only to find ridicule and disbelief. Today, I bear witness like so many others to the foreshadowing of the end of America as we know it. I am not prophesying doom and gloom for our nation, I am a man and do not know what the future holds in store for America. I can say that our way of life as defined by our founding fathers is on the verge of extinction. American Patriots are increasingly finding themselves pushed to the point in which the only option left for the salvation of this great Constitutional Republic is through force of arms. Even that may not produce the outcome hoped for. The forced importing of Islam and growing government protection for this ideology of hate; the flagrant disregard for constitutional law and procedure by all three branches of our government; the establishment of the Department of Homeland Security and its growing realm of authority; the intentional weakening of our armed forces; the growing force of global unity and community; all work together for the destruction of a way of life we have come to take for granted. While the fault lies with the complacency and lethargy of all Americans, the failure to maintain our Christian foundations rests only with the American Church. However, this booklet was not written to be an indictment upon the Church, it was written for one man to wrestle in finding his place as a committed follower of Jesus and an American Patriot in these changing and volatile times in America. And to take that understanding and communicate it to those who also face such difficult decisions in their life. The end is not here, but choices such as these must be made before the hardships are faced. That way your resolve for what is right is already established. A man who trains in peace, will be prepared for war.

I cannot express to you how I so desperately wanted to find justification in the Holy Scriptures to preserve these United States of America, honoring the Oath of Enlistment I took first as a soldier, then later as a United States Marine; being empowered to fulfill my deep patriotic love for

America and rise to her defense in her time of need. What I found instead was that every avenue of argument that I perused failed in such justification when laid next to right understanding of God's Holy Word. I thought that when I got to this point, because I knew deep in my heart that this would be my ultimate destination, that I would find sadness. Thinking that such sadness would rise up from the mourning that would follow. Being forced to make a choice between what is right before God and what is right before man. I do mourn, but not as one who has suffered loss, but as one who mourns those who struggle with this same issue and will choose to walk with the kingdom of men instead of what is right and true before God. For them my heart breaks, because they will find a way so that they can look themselves in the mirror and say "What I have done is right." We all must look in that mirror. The key is to ensure that deception is not standing there along side of us. I can only hope that I have communicated effectively in this endeavor. In addition, for those whom I love, who are American Patriots of the highest order, but are not followers of Christ, I hope you can now understand why my love for America has an apparent definitive boundary. It is not that I am a traitor to America, but that I am first a citizen of the Kingdom of God and in all good conscious must submit to what is excellent and not to what is temporal. It is my prayer that you too see the way of Christ as the supreme and most honorable of ways, joining us in a struggle that surpasses any struggle of earthly kingdoms. That is the struggle for all men to see the restoration of themselves to their creator through Jesus the Christ.

God bless you, *Michael "Mickey" Wilcox*

Be Blessed and Be the Blessing

Bibliography

> Constitution of the United States of America
> Deceleration of Independence
> A.C.L.U.
> Wikipedia
> The Washington Post – July 19, 2010 "A Hidden World Growing Beyond Control"
> The Platonist – article by Trivium August 28, 2009
> United Nations publications "Integrating Population Issues into Sustainable Development, including the 2015-post Development Agenda (Population Division of the Department of Economic and Social Affairs – United Nations)
> A Chronology of Quotes Regarding Centralized Power. Ed Thompson, March 2008
>Thomas Jefferson Quotes – National Debt Awareness Center
> Patriotic Quotes From American Christians. - Patrick LaJuett, 2015
> The Websters Dictionary
> The New International Version (Holy Bible)
> King James Version of the Holy Bible

<u>About the Author</u>

Michael "Mickey" Wilcox was
born in November of 1966 and surrendered his life to follow Jesus
wholeheartedly in April 2004. Before his willing embracing of Jesus,
he was deeply involved in the Boy Scouts of America, Civil Air Patrol
– Search and Rescue, and the U.S. Air Force Jr. R.O.T.C. Later he
served in the Pennsylvania Army National Guard with the 1/103rd
Armor Division. Eventually he went on to enlist active duty in the
United States Marine Corps where he was Honorably Discharged with
the rank of Corporal (E-4). While in the Marine Corps, he was
stationed at Marine Barracks Washington D.C. And then 6th Marines, 2
Mar. Div. Camp Lejeune N.C. Afterwards, trouble seemed to
accompany him throughout his life for the next many years until he
eventually found himself in trouble with the law. His life spiraled
downward filled with motorcycles, hard-partying and sometimes
violent living until the day Jesus interrupted his life. Since that day, he
has passionately and faithfully pursed the lifestyle of a true believer.
Speaking and expounding on the Gospel of Truth. As a published
author and traveled missionary both in the United States and abroad,
he has experienced the face of struggle and hardship up close. In his
zeal for the Lord, he has taken seriously the charge to share the
teachings of Jesus with all men.

To contact Mickey or schedule him to teach or present email him at:
usmc_mic@hotmail.com

The American Patriot & Christianity